The Assassination of Dr. Martin Luther King Jr.

Essential Events

THE ASSASSINATION OF
DR. MARTIN
LUTHER KING JR.
BY IDA WALKER

Content Consultant
Tenisha Armstrong, Associate Director
Martin Luther King Jr. Papers Project
Stanford University

ABDO
Publishing Company

CREDITS

Published by ABDO Publishing Company, 8000 West 78th Street, Edina, Minnesota 55439. Copyright © 2008 by Abdo Consulting Group, Inc. International copyrights reserved in all countries. No part of this book may be reproduced in any form without written permission from the publisher. The Essential Library™ is a trademark and logo of ABDO Publishing Company.

Printed in the United States.

Editor: Rebecca Rowell
Copy Editor: Paula Lewis
Interior Design and Production: Emily Love
Cover Design: Emily Love

Library of Congress Cataloging-in-Publication Data
Walker, Ida.
  The assassination of Dr. Martin Luther King Jr. / Ida Walker.
    p. cm. — (Essential events)
  Includes bibliographical references.
  ISBN 978-1-60453-044-5
  1. King, Martin Luther, Jr., 1929-1968—Assassination—Juvenile literature. I. Title.

  E185.97.K5W235 2008
  364.152'4092—dc22

                          2007031207

TABLE OF CONTENTS

Civil rights leader Martin Luther King Jr.

I See the
Promised Land

A solitary figure stood on the balcony outside room 306 of the Lorraine Motel in Memphis, Tennessee. Dr. Martin Luther King Jr. tried to take time each day to be alone just to contemplate. But those times of solitude and meditation were becoming increasingly rare. It seemed as though someone or something was always pulling at him, demanding his attention. But on this day, on the motel balcony, the civil rights leader had a few moments to himself.

King was extremely busy. He had been busy for a long time, working as a devoted advocate for civil rights for more than a decade. As the leader of the civil rights movement, his voice was the voice of many. African Americans wanted to end segregation and the unequal treatment they received in the United States. King spoke on their behalf, as well as for other minorities—including poor whites—and those who supported civil rights.

King's journey to Memphis had been a long one. For more than a century, African Americans had been treated by whites as though they were less than equal. In the South, African Americans and whites were physically segregated. Public places were divided into areas for blacks and those for whites. More than this, African Americans were often relegated to different opportunities than whites, including fewer job opportunities, lower pay, fewer educational opportunities, poorer schools, and fewer housing opportunities.

White Americans were divided on the issue of civil rights. In the South, segregation was a way of life. Many southerners thought segregation was acceptable because it was the only way they had experienced life. These southerners had been taught that blacks were not equal to whites and that separation of the two races was best. Other whites believed that segregation was wrong and that African Americans deserved the same opportunities as whites.

"It's all right to talk about long white robes over yonder, in all of its symbolism, but ultimately people want some suits and dresses and shoes to wear down here. It's all right to talk about streets flowing with milk and honey, but God has commanded us to be concerned about the slums down here and His children who can't eat three square meals a day."[1]

—*Martin Luther King Jr. from "I've been to the mountaintop," April 3, 1968, Memphis, Tennessee*

King lived with racism as a child, witnessing firsthand the social injustice of segregation. Growing up, he realized the importance of economic equality. After college and graduate school, King worked as a minister. He preached about civil rights and encouraged his parishioners to become members of the National Association for the Advancement of Colored People (NAACP). The more voices behind the movement, the stronger the movement would be. Over time and with his conviction, King's voice

A man exits a segregated bus terminal in Mississippi.

became stronger. He became the spokesperson of
the movement. He was a determined and dedicated
leader who advocated nonviolent protest. Regardless
of what they were faced with, protestors were
encouraged to remain peaceful.

Mahatma (Mohandas) Gandhi

Trained as a lawyer, Gandhi had spent many years helping Indians living in South Africa get their civil rights. Later, he returned to his native India and was the driving force in that country's move to independence from Great Britain. In all of his efforts, the leader insisted that his followers practice nonviolent civil disobedience. Despite the violent tactics used by those who opposed civil rights for Indians or independence for India, Gandhi and his followers held strong to their nonviolent protests and were triumphant in both arenas.

King admired the work of Mahatma (Mohandas) Gandhi, who believed in peaceful protest. Following Gandhi's example, King preached nonviolence. His campaign of civil disobedience brought him thousands of followers. Together, they protested throughout the South in places such as Montgomery, Birmingham, and Selma, Alabama. Each protest became a lesson for the next. The movement grew in size and strength, highlighted by the March on Washington for Jobs and Freedom, attended by more than 200,000 supporters. A federal law had even been passed in support of the cause: the Civil Rights Act of 1964.

King worked tirelessly for equality for all. His staff and supporters marveled at the 39-year-old's ability to maintain such a rigorous schedule of travel, speeches, and marches. King had much to do and was always on the go. He traveled from Washington, D.C., to Mississippi, to New York, to Georgia, and back to Washington. Now, he was in Memphis, Tennessee, because the African-American sanitation workers needed him.

THE MEMPHIS SANITATION WORKERS

The sanitation workers in Memphis struggled with poverty. Most of them earned less than two dollars a day—a month's wages were not enough to survive. Most of them were

Civil Disobedience

King believed in the power and effectiveness of civil disobedience, the nonviolent, purposeful violation of certain laws that a person believes are wrong. The modern idea of civil disobedience was developed by author Henry David Thoreau in his 1849 "Resistance to Civil Government," which is better known as "Civil Disobedience." As a form of protest against slavery and the Mexican-American War, Thoreau refused to pay taxes—a violation of federal law—and was jailed.

Mahatma Gandhi practiced civil disobedience in the early 1900s in his quest to help Indians gain their rights as citizens of India and their independence from the British government. Archbishop Desmond Tutu and Stephen Biko in South Africa used civil disobedience as a tool of protest, as did Rosa Parks, when she refused to give up her seat on a public bus in 1955 in Montgomery, Alabama.

Protestors generally expect to be arrested and taken to jail. While individuals who practice this form of protest vow not to use violence, law enforcement agents and others in power who confront these protestors are not always nonviolent. During the civil rights movement, many nonviolent protestors were met by powerful fire hose blasts, raging dogs, and nightsticks.

black, while the workers' supervisors were white. When work was called off because of bad weather, workers were sent home with two hours of pay. However, the supervisors received a full day of pay. When the African-American workers decided to strike, King went to Memphis to show his support.

On March 28, 1968, King traveled to Memphis to participate in a march in support of the black sanitation workers. The trip did not go well, beginning with his late arrival and ending with a riot.

Gandhi's Influence

King often looked to the words of Indian leader Gandhi when searching for the right words to address a crowd. While in Memphis, King again turned to his inspiration, saying, "Gandhi speaks for us: 'In the midst of death, life persists. In the midst of darkness, light persists.' We are today in the midst of death and darkness. We can strengthen life and live by our personal acts by saying 'no' to violence, by saying 'yes' to life."[2]

King left Memphis disappointed, but not defeated. He returned to Memphis a week later. Again, his arrival was delayed.

Late in the evening of April 3, 1968, King made his way to the pulpit of Bishop Charles Mason Temple. King had just sent Ralph Abernathy to speak that night. Abernathy arrived to television cameras and a crowd clearly there to see King. Abernathy called King at the Lorraine Motel, and King agreed to speak. An estimated 2,000 to 3,000 people had gathered. Most of those who attended were the striking sanitation workers. King reached the pulpit and, in the strong voice that many across the world had come to recognize and find inspirational, delivered what would become known as his "I've been to the mountaintop" speech. He said, "We mean business now, and we are determined to gain our rightful place in God's world."[3]

Speech Name

King's final speech is popularly known as the "I've been to the mountaintop" speech. It is also known by the title "I see the promised land." These titles come from standout phrases in the speech.

King's speeches often became more like sermons, and this one was no different. Those in the crowd became involved in the speech, with cries of "Amen" and "Hallelujah" echoing in the temple. As the subject of King's speech turned to his own life and the many threats that had been placed on it by his opponents, the crowd quieted:

We've got some difficult days ahead. But it doesn't matter with me now. Because I've been to the mountaintop. And I don't mind. Like anybody, I would like to live a long life. ... But I'm not concerned about that now. I just want to do God's will. And He's allowed me to go up to the mountain.

And I've looked over. And I've seen the promised land. I may not get there with you. But I want you to know tonight, that we, as a people, will get to the Promised Land. … I'm not worried about anything. I'm not fearing any man. Mine eyes have seen the glory of the coming of the Lord.[4]

King's voice rose and fell in a rhythm that mesmerized the audience. The crowd cheered and rose to their feet in appreciation, support, and love for this leader. Though the audience had no way of knowing it, this was to be King's last speech. Those in attendance would remember it for the rest of their lives. ⌐

King makes his last public appearance in Memphis.

King's birthplace in Atlanta, Georgia

YOUNG MARTIN

Martin Luther King Jr. was born in Atlanta, Georgia, on January 15, 1929. His mother, Alberta Williams King, worked briefly as a teacher before marrying Martin's father, Martin Luther King Sr. Martin's parents were devoted Christians. Mrs. King grew up in the church; her father was pastor of Ebenezer Baptist Church. He was succeeded as pastor by King Sr.

Martin was born during the Great Depression, a time when the American economy was dismal, and many Americans were unemployed and living in poverty. The middle-class King family did not have a lot of money, but Martin grew up in a nice home with all the food and clothes he needed. He also received a great deal of love and support. What he and other African Americans lacked were social equality and economic equality.

SEPARATE BUT NOT EQUAL

The world Martin entered was filled with restrictions on who he could be with and where he could go. When he was little, Martin had a white playmate. They had met when they were three years old. When the boys were old enough to go to school, they entered Atlanta's segregated school system. The white boy's father told him he could no longer play with Martin. Martin's parents tried to make him

Michael King

Martin Luther King Jr. was named Michael King when he was born. His birth certificate was filed on April 12, 1934, with the name Michael King. His birth certificate was altered to Martin Luther King Jr. on July 23, 1957. Under Georgia state law at the time, a legal name change was not required.

understand segregation and Martin realized there was a race problem in the United States. His parents taught him about the injustice of segregation with their words and actions.

Martin's father had long been an advocate for the rights of blacks in Atlanta. He boycotted buses after witnessing the beating of black bus passengers, he fought for equal salaries for black and white teachers, and he led efforts to eliminate the segregated elevators from the city's courthouse. As a child, Martin

Plessy v. Ferguson

Despite the Thirteenth and Fourteenth Amendments to the U.S. Constitution, blacks were not equal to whites in post-Civil War America. One area where the groups were segregated was public transportation. A group in Louisiana believed the practice was unfair; they decided to fight the state law that required blacks and whites to travel in separate railcars.

The group asked Homer Plessy to help them fight the law. Plessy agreed, and in 1892, he took a seat in a whites-only car of the East Louisiana Railroad. Because he was one-eighth black, Louisiana law stipulated that he was not entitled to ride in the car, even though his skin color was light. When he refused to leave the car, Plessy was arrested. He was fined $25.

After moving through the court system, Plessy's appeal reached the U.S. Supreme Court. In the 7–1 decision, the Court ruled that as long as accommodations were equal in quality, the races could be segregated. And since there seemed to be no difference in quality between the cars for white passengers and those for black passengers, the lower court ruling was upheld.

Later, the ruling was expanded to cover other cases, such as public schools. Even organizations that had integrated, such as the federal government, reestablished segregation policies as a result of expanded Plessy rulings.

learned from his father the lessons that would lead to his role in the civil rights movement.

Martin also learned an important lesson from his mother. Mrs. King explained segregation to Martin and that separate did not mean less than or unequal to anyone. Instead, she told her son, "You are as good as anyone."[I]

Martin the Student

Martin attended segregated schools: Yonge Street Elementary School, David T. Howard Elementary School, Atlanta University Laboratory School, and Booker T. Washington High School. He was a good student. He even skipped two grades.

At 14, Martin took part in an oratorical contest in Dublin, Georgia. He traveled to Dublin by bus with a teacher, Mrs. Bradley. Martin won the contest with his

Jim Crow Laws

Passed in the late 1800s and early 1900s, Jim Crow laws were established by Southern states to separate African Americans and whites socially. These laws affected all areas of life. For example, in Alabama:

• The conductor of each passenger train had to assign each passenger to the appropriate section of cars divided into areas designated for specific races.

• Whites and blacks were not allowed to be served in the same room of a restaurant unless the room was physically divided by a partition at least seven feet (2 m) high and there was a separate entrance from the street to each area.

• It was illegal for blacks and whites to play pool or billiards together.

The term "Jim Crow" comes from a song of the same name performed by a white actor in blackface makeup who performed a stereotypical black character in an exaggerated manner.

speech, "The negro and the constitution," in which
he said:

> We cannot have an enlightened democracy with one great
> group living in ignorance. We cannot have a healthy nation
> with one-tenth of the people ill-nourished, sick, harboring
> germs of disease which recognize no color lines. ...We cannot
> have a nation orderly and sound with one group so ground
> down and thwarted that it is almost forced into unsocial
> attitudes and crime. We cannot be truly Christian people so
> long as we flout the central teachings of Jesus: brotherly love
> and the Golden Rule. We cannot come to full prosperity with
> one great group so ill-delayed that it cannot buy goods. So as
> we gird ourselves to defend democracy from foreign attack, let
> us see to it that increasingly at home we give fair play and free
> opportunity for all people.[2]

During the ride home, Martin's joy over winning
the contest turned to anger. When the bus picked
up white passengers, the bus driver ordered Martin
and his teacher to give up their seats to the white
passengers. When the two did not move as quickly as
the bus driver wanted, he began yelling and cursing
at them. Martin and Mrs. Bradley rode 90 miles
(145 km) to Atlanta standing in the aisle of the bus.
Martin wrote later of the experience that it was "the

This sign at a Greyhound station is one example of segregation in the South.

angriest I have ever been in my life."[3] He had just won a prize for his speech about the rights of African Americans but was not allowed to keep his seat on a bus. The experience shaped his understanding of injustice and the leader he would one day become.

BECOMING A MINISTER

Like most teenagers, Martin did not really know what he wanted to do with his life. He knew he wanted to help people, but he was not sure how best to do it. However, he was sure of one thing: he did not want to become a minister. Martin was religious, but he thought that religion was not intellectually respectable. Martin thought he could best help people by becoming a lawyer or a doctor.

Like his father and grandfather, Martin attended Morehouse College in Atlanta. After passing a special admissions test, he entered Morehouse in September 1944 at the age of 15. Martin studied Henry David Thoreau, a nineteenth-century author who wrote about the role of the individual in changing laws. Thoreau believed that it was all right to break an unjust law. To protest the Mexican-American War and slavery, Thoreau refused to pay taxes and was jailed. Martin liked the idea of nonviolent resistance. His interest in political and social issues grew.

While at Morehouse, Martin's attitude toward religion changed. Two of his professors were ministers, and they influenced Martin with their talk about battling racial discrimination, poverty, and hunger. Dr. Benjamin Elijah Mays was president of Morehouse College. Dr. George Kelsey was a professor of philosophy and religion. Through these mentors, Martin saw his ideal for a minister: a man who was deeply religious and a modern thinker.

After graduating from Morehouse in 1948 with a degree in sociology, Martin attended Crozer Theological Seminary, a small school in Pennsylvania. While at Crozer, Martin studied the life and work of Mahatma Gandhi, who had promoted nonviolence as a form of protest, including boycotts of British products and establishments. Gandhi's work fit well with Thoreau's practice of civil disobedience. In his own life as a leader, Martin would follow Thoreau's and Gandhi's practices.

On May 8, 1951, Martin earned a second degree, graduating with a bachelor of divinity from Crozer. He then decided to pursue a graduate degree in theology. He entered Boston University's School of Theology in the fall of 1951. His

Morehouse College

Morehouse College is one of the most prestigious historically black colleges in the United States. The school was founded in Augusta, Georgia, in 1867 as the Augusta Institute by William Jefferson White, a Baptist minister; Reverend Richard C. Coulter, a former slave; and Reverend Edmund Turney of the National Theological Institute in Washington, D.C. The school moved to Atlanta in 1879 and was renamed the Atlanta Baptist Seminary. In 1897, the name changed to Atlanta Baptist College. The school took Morehouse College as its name in 1913 in honor of Henry L. Morehouse, who was affiliated with the Northern Baptist Home Mission Society.

Since its beginning, Morehouse College has earned the reputation as an academically focused school. The all-male school expects the men who attend it to concentrate on their education, though students can participate in intercollegiate sports.

Brown v. Board of Education

In 1896, *Plessy v. Ferguson* established the "separate but equal" doctrine used to segregate public schools. The schools and academic opportunities for black children were often inferior to those for white children. *Brown v. Board of Education* was filed by the NAACP in Topeka, Kansas, on behalf of 13 parents who wanted equal opportunities for their children. The case focused on the fact that, while black schools in Topeka had equal facilities and teacher salaries, programs and textbooks were not equally available. In addition, there were 18 elementary schools for whites but only four for blacks, making attending a neighborhood school impossible for blacks.

The district court ruled in favor of the school board. The NAACP appealed to the U.S. Supreme Court. The case was argued by Thurgood Marshall and other NAACP lawyers in December 1952 and reargued a year later. The Court overturned *Plessy* on May 17, 1954.

life would soon change in a new way: he would fall in love.

Coretta Scott

Coretta Scott was born on April 27, 1927, in rural Alabama. She grew up in a poor, hardworking farm family. Her parents were determined to sacrifice so that their children could receive an education. Coretta took advantage of the opportunities her parents provided for her. She graduated at the top of her high school class. A scholarship made it possible for her to attend Antioch College in Ohio.

In addition to studying music and majoring in elementary education at Antioch, Coretta joined the local branch of the NAACP and various race-relations committees at the college. She had learned about prejudice and lack of rights in Alabama. While she and other students walked five miles

(8 km) to a one-room school for black students, buses carrying white students to a nearby all-white school passed them by.

Coretta graduated from Antioch and received a scholarship to the prestigious New England Conservatory of Music in Boston. She met Martin in January 1952. On June 18, 1953, Martin and Coretta married in Marion, Alabama, Coretta's hometown. The ceremony was performed by Martin's father.

RETURNING TO THE SOUTH

After Coretta earned her degree in voice and music education from the New England Conservatory of Music in 1954, the young couple returned to the South when they moved to Montgomery, Alabama. Martin still had some work to do before he would receive his doctoral degree, but he had completed the requirement that he physically attend Boston University. Martin received offers to serve at churches and to teach at various universities. Eager to return to the South, Martin accepted the offer to become the minister at the Dexter Avenue Baptist Church. Martin and Coretta's desire to return to the South was strong, and they felt this opportunity was too good to pass up.

Martin served Dexter Avenue Baptist Church for five years. This church was his only full-time pastorate. Church membership grew as the new minister preached about saving souls and helping with more earthly concerns such as education, jobs, and voting. Most of his congregation could relate to those issues, and they supported their young pastor and his family. These concerns seemed innocent and basic. But some people in Alabama, the rest of the South, and the United States agreed only partially. Many felt the rights to receive a good education, to have a decent job, and to vote were good only for a certain group of people: whites. For others, especially African Americans, it was almost as though they should be satisfied with what they had. Many others, however, including Martin, could not disagree more. He was not going to stand still and let things be. ⌒

Family

Martin and Coretta King would eventually have four children: Yolanda, Martin III, Dexter, and Bernice.

Martin and Coretta with three of their four children in 1963

During segregation, African-American passengers were required to sit at the back of buses.

Becoming a Leader

ing's interest in social and political change continued after he returned to the South. Not long after moving to Montgomery, he was drawn into the organized civil rights movement.

On December 1, 1955, Rosa Parks boarded a
bus in Montgomery for the ride home after a day of
work. She took a seat in the middle of the bus. The
bus soon became crowded. When white passengers
were left standing in the aisle,
Parks remained in her seat rather
than follow the law that said blacks
had to give up their seats to white
riders. The bus driver called the
police. When officers arrived, Parks
refused to move. She was arrested.

Civil rights leader E.D.
Nixon was pleased with the arrest
because he had been looking for
a court case to fight the law that
allowed segregation on public
transportation. With Parks, he
found his fight. With this case, he
would also find a leader for the civil
rights movement.

MONTGOMERY IMPROVEMENT ASSOCIATION

King had preached about civil
rights in many of his sermons

Learning to Fight Segregation

For many who wanted
to fight segregation and
other forms of preju-
dice, the first step was to
learn how. Thousands of
African Americans and
whites learned how by
attending the Highlander
Folk School in Tennessee.
The school was founded
in 1932 by Myles Horton,
a white former theology
student, and Don West, a
native Georgian.

In addition to teach-
ing individuals how to
use nonviolent methods
to combat prejudice, in
the 1950s, the school ran
Citizenship Schools in the
South. The schools taught
African Americans how
to read and write, giving
them the tools they need-
ed to register to vote.

Renamed Highlander
Research and Education
Center, the organization
continues to provide leadership training.

at Dexter Avenue Baptist Church. He even demanded that all congregation members join the NAACP. King was active in learning about and addressing current social issues. Not long after Parks was arrested, Nixon pushed for a boycott of Montgomery's buses by the city's blacks, an idea that had been promoted for a couple of years by Jo Ann Robinson and other members of the Women's Political Council. Nixon contacted King about getting involved in the boycott. He also discussed a boycott with Ralph Abernathy, minister of the First Baptist Church. The three men exchanged many phone calls discussing a boycott. King offered to hold the meeting at his church.

During that and subsequent meetings, the community's African-American ministers met and defined their plan of action. The men formed the Montgomery Improvement Association (MIA), and King was chosen to lead the organization.

"We Are American Citizens"

The one-day bus boycott proved successful, but MIA members believed more action was needed to bring about change. Before calling for a longer boycott, they wanted to find out if the community would stand behind it. More than 1,000 people attended a meeting to hear the MIA's plans. King, nervous and unfamiliar to many in the audience, stood at the pulpit. He spoke of Rosa Parks's courage and the courage of those who faced discrimination based on race:

> [F]irst and foremost, we are American citizens ... we are not here advocating violence. ... We have never done that. The only weapon that we have ... is the weapon of protest. ... the great glory of American democracy is the right to protest for right. ... Not only are we using the tools of persuasion, but we've ... got to use the tools of coercion. Not only is this thing a process of education, but it is also a process of legislation.[1]

The audience gave King a standing ovation. They were ready to follow him into nonviolent battle. A movement and a leader were born.

"And as we stand and sit here this evening and as we prepare ourselves for what lies ahead, let us go out with the grim and bold determination that we are going to stick together. We are going to work together. Right here in Montgomery, when the history books are written in the future, somebody will have to say, 'There lived a race of people, a black people, "fleecy locks and black complexion," a people who had the moral courage to stand up for their rights. And thereby they injected a new meaning into the veins of history and of civilization.' And we're going to do that. God grant that we will do it before it is too late. As we proceed with our program, let us think of these things."[2]

—Martin Luther King Jr.
Address to the
MIA Mass Meeting,
December 5, 1955,
Montgomery, Alabama

Walking for Equal Rights

During the longer bus boycott, King and an army of volunteers—blacks and whites—worked to get blacks to their jobs, schools, and churches without buses. Boycotters tried to remain firm in following King's plea for nonviolence. It was not easy, though, when walkers were threatened, had things thrown at them, or were chased. King was also attacked.

On January 30, 1956, King's house was bombed. Coretta and their newborn daughter, Yolanda, were inside when the bomb exploded on the porch. The house was damaged, but no one was hurt. When word reached King, he and others at a meeting quickly went to the house. A crowd that had gathered on the street started to get out of control. Many called for retaliation.

As King came out of his home and told the crowd that everyone inside was safe and had not been hurt, he pleaded that nonviolence not be abandoned, saying,

> We believe in law and order. Don't get panicky. ... Don't get your weapons. ... We are not advocating violence. We want to love our enemies. I want you to love our enemies. Be good to them. Love them and let them know you love them.

I did not start this boycott. I was asked by you to serve as your spokesman. I want it to be known the length and breadth of this land that if I am stopped this movement will not stop. If I am stopped our work will not stop. For what we are doing is right. What we are doing is just. And God is with us.[3]

The crowd responded with support and calmly left.

After the bombing and indictment, King's father asked him to return to Atlanta for his family's safety. King Sr. even asked the presidents of Morehouse and Atlanta

The Early Civil Rights Movement

One of the first institutions to try to help blacks achieve equality in a white world was the black church. Blacks could find support, information, financial resources, and even dispute resolution programs within their churches. During the early civil rights movement, most churches did not become involved with the political side of issues, but they did help their members with the practical side of life.

The National Association for the Advancement of Colored People (NAACP) was created in 1909. The influential black leader W.E.B. Du Bois edited the NAACP's magazine and was the public face of the organization. The NAACP worked hard to fight Jim Crow laws in the courts and to make the general public aware of the issues faced by African Americans.

The Universal Negro Improvement Association (UNIA) was formed in 1914 by Marcus Garvey, a publisher, orator, and journalist. Unlike most civil rights groups of the time, the UNIA was not looking to integrate blacks into white society. Instead, it looked toward helping blacks achieve economic freedom despite the segregated society. The UNIA and Marcus Garvey are best known for the "back to Africa" movement, which encouraged blacks in America to return to Africa, specifically Liberia.

Browder v. Gayle

While Rosa Parks is well-known in the United States, few people know of Aurelia Browder, Susie McDonald, Claudette Colvin, and Mary Louise Smith. Their case ended the segregation of public transportation in Montgomery, Alabama. Jeanetta Reese was originally included in the case, but she dropped out because of threats of economic retaliation and violence.

The case was filed by attorney Fred Gray. He believed the 1954 ruling in *Brown v. Board of Education* applied to public transportation. In *Brown*, the U.S. Supreme Court had determined that segregation was not acceptable, even if races had the same opportunities, just in different facilities. The district court agreed with Gray, as did the U.S. Supreme Court.

Alabama appealed the ruling, which the Court rejected on December 17, 1956. On December 20, the Court forced Alabama officials to adhere to the ruling.

University to convince his son to leave Montgomery. They did not succeed.

FIGHTING SEGREGATION IN COURT

On February 1, 1956, a case was filed against the bus company and the city in district court on behalf of four women who had been charged under Montgomery's transportation segregation laws. In June, the court ruled in favor of the four women. The case was appealed to the U.S. Supreme Court.

While waiting for the Court's decision, the boycott continued and lasted for more than a year. During that time, the city tried using arrests to stop the protest. Along with thousands of other protestors, King was charged with various minor offenses. In February 1956, 89 boycotters, including King, were indicted for violating a 1921 state law barring conspiracies that interfered with lawful businesses. King's trial began in March. He was found guilty and sentenced to a fine of $500 plus court costs or 386 days of hard labor. He was released on bond.

On November 13, 1956, the Supreme Court agreed with the district court ruling, calling the local laws pertaining to segregation on public transportation unconstitutional. On December 20, federal injunctions were officially served to those who ran the bus company, the officials of the city of Montgomery, and Alabama state officials integrating the buses. On December 21, 1956, after 381 days of boycotting, African Americans began riding the Montgomery buses again. They were now free to sit wherever they wanted.

The dedication and determination of thousands of Montgomery citizens made the boycott a success. The city's public transportation was now integrated. And it had been done with nonviolent protests.

"I want you to know that if M.L. King had never been born this movement would have taken place. I just happened to be here. You know there comes a time when time itself is ready for change. That time has come in Montgomery, and I had nothing to do with it."[4]

—Martin Luther King Jr.
MIA Mass Meeting,
January 30, 1956

NATIONAL ATTENTION

The Montgomery bus boycott received national attention. Both the Supreme Court ruling and King's indictment and trial helped the civil rights movement. The event attracted the attention of the national press. Organizations nationwide contacted King to address their meetings. In August 1956, he spoke before the platform committee of the Democratic Party, trying to ensure that civil rights issues would be part of the campaign of the Democratic nominee for president of the United States. King received national attention when his photo appeared on the covers of *Time* magazine and the *New York Times Magazine* and in newspapers nationwide. He was interviewed by print, television, and radio reporters. King and his cause were now famous. ⌐

Ralph Abernathy, left, and Martin Luther King Jr.

King, second from left, and other civil rights leaders begin the march from Selma to Montgomery, Alabama.

I HAVE A DREAM

The Montgomery bus boycott was only a small advance in the civil rights movement. More work was needed to end segregation and to create economic and social equality between blacks and whites in the United States.

SOUTHERN CHRISTIAN LEADERSHIP CONFERENCE

The Montgomery bus boycott inspired supporters in other cities. Spread of the movement would be most effective if it were coordinated. Bayard Rustin organized a meeting for January 10, 1957, in Atlanta. He invited dozens of southern black leaders, most of them ministers. The men formed what would become the Southern Christian Leadership Conference (SCLC), to coordinate the actions of local protest groups. King became the group's leader.

The SCLC taught protestors the Christian nonviolence King advocated. The movement grew in size and strength.

PRAYER PILGRIMAGE

On May 17, 1957, the Prayer Pilgrimage for Freedom was held in Washington, D.C., to commemorate the third anniversary of *Brown v. Board of Education.* Thousands of Americans—blacks and whites—came from across the country to show their support. A three-hour service was held at the Lincoln Memorial. The

Crusade for Citizenship

The SCLC planned the Crusade for Citizenship for the summer of 1957. The goal of the crusade was the enforcement of voting rights for African Americans.

The SCLC

Founded in 1957, the SCLC strives to end racial injustice through nonviolent means. The organization has local chapters across the United States that work on a variety of projects, including voter registration and education, conflict resolution and nonviolence training, economic empowerment, health care, youth development, and collegiate chapter development.

event aimed to raise the nation's awareness of racial justice issues.

Youth Groups

Many young people took on the civil rights cause. In 1960, hundreds of African-American college student leaders founded a youth organization called the Student Nonviolent Coordinating Committee (SNCC).

SNCC conducted the same types of protests as the SCLC. The group formed as the result of a sit-in at a Woolworth's lunch counter in Greensboro, North Carolina. Four black college students sat at the counter until the store closed. Twenty black students returned the next day to continue the sit-in. The number of protestors increased daily until hundreds of students were taking part in the sit-in at Woolworth's and other stores.

SNCC energized the movement. Sit-ins were held by thousands of students in dozens of cities. SNCC was not the only activist group with college students. The Congress of Racial Equality (CORE) included white college students from northern

states. Similar to SNCC, CORE protested with sit-
ins and demonstrations.

CORE also led "freedom rides." In 1946, the
Supreme Court ruled that segregating buses and
trains traveling between states was illegal. In 1960,
the Court ruled segregation in transportation
facilities unconstitutional. In 1961, CORE sent
"freedom riders" throughout the South to ride buses
and go into terminals. In May of 1961, 18 volunteers
ranging in age from 17 to 61 tested the ruling.
Black volunteers used white-only facilities, while
white volunteers used black facilities. They might
be arrested, abused, or both. They
were ready to sacrifice themselves
for the cause and without violence.
Their work resulted in new rules
that forced integration on buses
and in bus terminals.

BIRMINGHAM

The fight against segregation
was particularly difficult in
Birmingham, Alabama. Fred
Shuttlesworth, president of the
Alabama Christian Movement

Civil Rights Organizations

The SCLC was one of several organizations that fought for justice and equality during the civil rights movement. Other organizations include:
• Congress of Racial Equality (CORE)
• Leadership Conference on Civil Rights
• National Association for the Advancement of Colored People (NAACP)
• National Urban League
• Student Nonviolent Co-ordinating Committee SNCC)

for Human Rights and SCLC secretary, invited King to Birmingham. King and the SCLC worked with Shuttlesworth on the Birmingham campaign. Together, they planned "Project C" (*C* for *confrontation*) to take place around Easter of 1963.

The plan targeted Birmingham businesses. SCLC volunteers would stage sit-ins at lunch counters and stores. Easter was a busy time for retailers. Store sit-ins would interfere with shoppers and limit storeowners' profits. Hundreds of protestors were arrested during the first few days of Project C. More arrests would come.

The next phase of the

SNCC Conference

On April 15, 1960, King spoke at the founding of SNCC, noting that the group must develop a strategy:

Some elements which suggest themselves for discussion are: (1) The need for some type of continuing organization. ... (2) ... A nationwide campaign of "selective buying."... It is immoral to spend one's money where one cannot be treated with respect. (3) ... Training a group of volunteers who will willingly go to jail rather than pay bail or fines. ... We are in an era in which a prison term for a freedom struggle is a badge of honor. (4) The youth must take the freedom struggle into every community in the South without exception. ... (5) The students will certainly want to delve deeper into the philosophy of nonviolence. ... resistance and nonviolence are not in themselves good. There is another element that must be present in our struggle that then makes our resistance and nonviolence truly meaningful. That element is reconciliation. Our ultimate end must be the creation of the beloved community.[1]

plan was demonstrations. Marches were held daily. A court ordered that the demonstrations stop. King announced that he would lead a march through the city. The protestors were arrested and jailed, including King, who was placed in solitary confinement.

Eight white Alabama clergymen published a statement on April 12, 1963, denouncing King and asking him to stop the protests. King responded on April 16 with his now-famous "Letter from Birmingham Jail," writing,

> *I am in Birmingham because injustice is here. … Injustice anywhere is a threat to justice everywhere. … It is unfortunate that demonstrations are taking place in Birmingham, but it is even more unfortunate that the city's white power structure left the Negro community with no alternative.* [2]

King was released from jail on April 20, but this was not the end to protests in Birmingham. A "Children's Crusade" took place in early May. African-American youth took to the streets of Birmingham to protest segregation and support civil rights. Officers sprayed water on the children with fire hoses and unleashed dogs to attack them. More than 1,000 young people were arrested.

Martin Luther King Jr., 1961

Even with arrests, jailing, beatings, and attacks, Project C was a success. It unified African Americans nationwide in support of desegregation. It was also a moral victory. The protestors never gave up and never gave in to violence. Finally, an agreement was reached on May 10 that laid out plans for desegregating Birmingham and hiring more blacks. The Birmingham protest in 1963 resulted in great progress in the fight for equality.

MARCH ON WASHINGTON FOR JOBS AND FREEDOM

President Kennedy was fully aware of the struggle of African Americans as a result of segregation. King and Kennedy communicated regularly, especially during the Birmingham protests. The violence witnessed by Americans during the protests prompted Kennedy to address the issue of civil rights. On June 11, 1963, he announced a civil rights bill in an address to the nation, saying,

> We face … a moral crisis as a country and a people … it is time to act. The events in Birmingham and elsewhere have so increased the cries for equality that no city or state or legislative body can prudently choose to ignore them.[3]

On June 19, he presented the bill to Congress for approval.

Civil rights leaders organized a massive demonstration in Washington, D.C., to show support of Kennedy's proposed bill. The March on Washington for Jobs and Freedom was held on August 28. Marchers demanded that the civil rights bill be passed, schools and housing be desegregated, job training be provided, and the minimum wage be increased. Standing at the foot of the Lincoln Memorial, King gave the final speech of the day:

I have a dream that one day this nation will rise up and live out the true meaning of its creed. "We hold these truths to be self-evident, that all men are created equal."...

I have a dream that one day even the state of Mississippi, a state sweltering with the heat of injustice, sweltering with the heat of oppression, will be transformed into an oasis of freedom and justice.

I have a dream that my four little children will one day live in a nation where they will not be judged by the color of their skin but by the content of their character. [4]

King concluded his speech with words that have become perhaps his most famous, "Free at last! Free at last! Thank God Almighty, we are free at last!"[5]

More than 200,000 people gathered to show their support of the movement and hundreds of thousands more viewed the event on television.

Selma, Alabama

King was keenly aware of the need for all African Americans to not only have the right to vote but actually be able to vote. Many in the South were denied their right to vote by local laws that discriminated against black citizens. This included literacy tests that many poor, uneducated southern African Americans could not pass.

The SCLC chose Selma, Alabama, as the center of its voter discrimination campaign. Fewer than 350 of the 15,000 eligible black voters there were registered to vote. The SCLC, the Dallas County Voters League, and SNCC conducted a voter registration drive and demonstrations in Selma. A state trooper in the nearby town of Marion responded with violence, fatally shooting resident protestor Jimmie Lee Jackson. Local activists planned a march for March 7, 1965, in Jackson's honor from Selma to Montgomery.

The march included crossing the Edmund Pettus Bridge. State troopers and local police blocked the far side of the bridge. The marchers were met with billy clubs and tear gas, and they were chased by the troopers. The assault, known as "Bloody Sunday," was televised nationally. Another march was called for March 9. That morning, a judge ordered that the protest be barred until a federal hearing was held. King led the second march. He took the marchers to the site of "Bloody Sunday," asked them to pray, and then marched back to Selma.

1964 Civil Rights Act

Kennedy did not live to see his civil rights bill become law. He was assassinated on November 22, 1963. Upon becoming president, Lyndon Johnson steered the bill through Congress in July 1964. The 1964 Civil Rights Act made racial discrimination in public places illegal and required employers to provide equal employment opportunities. The law also gave the U.S. attorney general the power to bring legal action anywhere there was a pattern of resistance to the law.

A third march was planned after a federal court approved it. Protestors left Selma on March 21, protected by 1,800 National Guardsmen on the 54-mile (87-km) trek. They arrived at Montgomery four days later. Approximately 25,000 people attended the rally, led by King, who said,

> *The end we seek is a society at peace with itself, a society that can live with its conscience. ... I know you are asking today, "How long will it take?" ... however difficult the moment, however frustrating the hour, it will not be long.*[6]

There was no mistaking King's dedication or the conviction of the thousands of supporters who wanted equality for all Americans. There was also no mistaking the fact that not everyone believed in the civil rights movement.

Civil rights supporters march in Selma, Alabama, in March 1965.

After being arrested, King, right, and Abernathy are booked by a police officer in Montgomery, Alabama.

WE SHALL OVERCOME

Throughout the civil rights movement, demonstrators were met with anger, hate, and even violence. Singing helped protestors unite and meet their many challenges with greater strength. "We Shall Overcome" became the theme song of the civil rights movement. It could have been considered the mantra for King and his followers in their everyday lives.

First Arrest

During the Montgomery bus boycott, King experienced the ugliness of racism from officials and citizens alike. An easy way for officials to try to stop King and his supporters was through citations and arrests—often for minor or made-up offenses. King was arrested repeatedly during his years of supporting civil rights. He was jailed for the first time in Montgomery on January 26, 1956. The charge was speeding. He was fined $14.

King also received threatening telephone calls and letters because of Montgomery—sometimes dozens a day. In late January 1956, one caller said, "Listen ... we've taken all we want from you; before next week you'll be sorry you ever came to Montgomery."[1] On the evening of January 30, a bomb exploded on the porch of King's home. No one was hurt, but bombings would continue throughout the movement—some would prove deadly.

"Man's inhumanity to man is not only perpetrated by the vitriolic [hateful] actions of those who are bad. It is also perpetrated by the vitiating [impairing] inaction of those who are good."[2]

—*Martin Luther King Jr.*

King and the FBI

Opposition even came from federal authorities

"We Shall Overcome"

Songs united the thousands fighting for civil rights. "We Shall Overcome" became the movement's unofficial anthem. The lyrics come from "I'll Overcome Some Day," a gospel song written in 1900. Part of the melody comes from the spiritual "No More Auction Block for Me." The song has seven verses. Its chorus is sung after each verse.

Chorus: Oh, deep in my heart, I do believe, We shall overcome some day

1. We shall overcome, We shall overcome, We shall overcome some day

2. We'll walk hand in hand, We'll walk hand in hand, We'll walk hand in hand some day

3. We shall all be free, We shall all be free, We shall all be free some day

4. We are not afraid, We are not afraid, We are not afraid some day

5. We are not alone, We are not alone, We are not alone some day

6. The whole wide world around, The whole wide world around, The whole wide world around some day

7. We shall overcome, We shall overcome, We shall overcome some day[3]

such as the Federal Bureau of Investigation (FBI). Under the leadership of FBI Director J. Edgar Hoover and with authorization by U.S. Attorney General Robert Kennedy, agents wiretapped King's home and office. This allowed the FBI to listen in on King's private conversations. The wiretapping was part of the secret surveillance Hoover placed on King. Hoover, known to be racist, believed

King was a communist. In 1956, Hoover established COINTELPRO. This program went beyond watching King to going undercover into civil rights groups, interfering with group activities, and trying to give the groups a bad reputation. Because King was the leader of the civil rights movement, Hoover and the FBI paid particular attention to him. For some in government, such as Hoover, King's continuing growth as a leader was seen as threatening and something to be stopped.

ATTACKED IN NEW YORK

Autumn 1958 was particularly challenging for King. His first book, *Stride Toward Freedom: The Montgomery Story*, was published in September. It told his story of the Montgomery bus boycott. While at a book signing at a Harlem store in New York City on September 20, King was stabbed by Izola Ware Curry, a mentally ill black woman. Even this event did not sway his thinking about the goodness of people. Upon wakening after surgery, King said of his attacker,

King as Author

In 1958, King's first book was published. *Stride Toward Freedom: The Montgomery Story* told the story of the Montgomery bus boycott. The book was the first of several written by King. Other titles include:

- *Why We Can't Wait*
- *Measure of a Man*
- *Strength to Love*
- *Where Do We Go from Here: Chaos or Community?*

"This person needs help. She is not responsible for the violence she has done me. Don't do anything to her; don't prosecute her. Get her healed."[4]

Tax Evasion

While King was arrested repeatedly during the movement, not all of the charges against him were because of his protesting. Some were filed against him simply to cause him harm, including imprisoning him for long periods of time.

On February 17, 1960, King was arrested for tax evasion. "The white Southern power structure … indicted me for perjury and openly proclaimed that I would be imprisoned for at least ten years."[5] He was charged with providing false information on his 1956 and 1958 Alabama state tax returns. He stood trial for three days before a white judge, a white prosecutor, and an all-white Southern jury. The situation did not look good.

The courtroom was segregated. Passions were inflamed. Feelings ran high. The press and other communications media were hostile. Defeat seemed certain, and we in the freedom struggle braced ourselves for the inevitable.[6]

The jury found King innocent of the charges.

King was arrested several times throughout the civil rights movement.

FREEDOM RIDERS ATTACKED

Violence occurred in all kinds of places, including public facilities. On May 4, 1961, freedom riders boarded buses to ride to the South. Protestors included James Farmer, CORE's founder. On May 14, freedom riders encountered trouble in Birmingham, where they were met by an angry crowd. Some of the freedom riders were beaten. Freedom riders in Anniston and Montgomery were also attacked. A bus in Anniston was set on fire. As in Birmingham, freedom riders in both Anniston and

Freedom riders faced attack in Alabama in May 1961 in their fight for civil rights.

Montgomery were beaten. New members took the places of those who were hurt or arrested. No matter what they encountered, the freedom riders did not retaliate. They remained peaceful.

More Violence

In the years that followed, even as King and the thousands of others who supported civil rights protested peacefully, opponents continued to respond with verbal and physical abuse. There was no limit to the destruction and harm some civil rights opponents would cause.

On the evening of June 12, 1963, Medgar Evers was killed. Evers worked for the NAACP in Mississippi and helped African Americans register to vote. He was shot to death in his driveway.

Deaths were not limited to civil rights leaders. On September 15, four black girls were killed in an explosion in Birmingham. Civil rights meetings were often held at Sixteenth Street Baptist Church. Though the bomb went off in an empty basement, the brick and glass sent flying by the explosion went into a nearby classroom filled with children. Addie Mae Collins, 14, Denise McNair, 11, Carole Robertson, 14, and Cynthia Wesley, 14, died as a result of the blast.

On the evening of March 9, 1965, James Reeb, a white minister from Massachusetts who had traveled to Selma to take part in the protest, was beaten by several white men. He died two days later. President Johnson held a press conference on March 15, 1965, saying,

Responding with Violence

The nonviolence King advocated came to an end with the bombing of the Sixteenth Street Baptist Church in Birmingham. Some blacks expressed their anger about the bombing with violence and rioting. Others called for calm but to no avail. The ensuing riots and violence resulted in two deaths. A 16-year-old black youth was shot and killed by police, and a 13-year-old black youth was killed by two white youth.

Johnson's Reaction

In addition to holding a press conference in response to James Reeb's death, President Johnson called Reeb's widow and father to express his condolences. Many civil rights leaders were disappointed in Johnson for not responding similarly to Jimmie Lee Jackson's death just days before. Johnson did not reach out to Jackson's family.

It is wrong to do violence to peaceful citizens in the streets of their town. It is wrong to deny Americans the right to vote. It is wrong to deny any person full equality because of the color of his skin.[7]

FIGHTING WITH LOVE

No matter what King was confronted with—citations, arrests, threats, or violence—King responded peacefully. He believed love was the way to change:

Along the way of life, someone must have sense enough and morality enough to cut off the chain of hate and evil. The greatest way to do that is through love. I believe firmly that love is a transforming power that can lift a whole community to new horizons of fair play, good-will, and justice.[8]

But King's love and understanding could not change everything. He would meet retaliation that was impossible to overcome.

King received the Nobel Prize for Peace in December 1964 for his nonviolent protests for civil rights. He donated his prize winnings to the movement.

The drive-in sign at the Lorraine Motel in Memphis, Tennessee

SHOTS FIRED

King wanted all people in the United States to have economic equality. He believed all races would not be equal until everyone had the same economic opportunities. Many members of the black community lived in extreme poverty. King thought those impoverished conditions prevented blacks and other minorities from achieving equality in all aspects of their lives.

The black sanitation workers in Memphis, Tennessee, struggled with poverty. Most of them earned less than two dollars a day. A black sanitation worker in Memphis could work an entire month and still have an income low enough to be eligible for food stamps and other public assistance programs. It rained constantly in Memphis. On rainy days, workers—most of them black—were dismissed with only two hours of pay. With so many rainy days, workers' already meager wages were even less. Meanwhile, the workers' superiors, who were white, were paid full wages, rain or shine. The black workers, nearly 1,300 in number, called a strike.

In March 1968, King was on a tight schedule. Even so, some of King's advisors wanted him to go to Memphis in support of the strike called by the black sanitation workers. Others, including his trusted aide, Andrew Young, were against the trip. The presidential race was in full swing, and King

"We have moved into an era where we are called upon to raise certain basic questions about the whole society. We are still called upon to give aid to the beggar who finds himself in misery and agony on life's highway. But one day, we must ask the question of whether an edifice which produces beggars must not be restructured and refurbished. That is where we are now."[1]

—*Martin Luther King Jr.*

Launched on December 4, 1967, the Poor People's Campaign was the second phase of the civil rights movement. The first phase of the movement "exposed the problems of segregation through nonviolence." King's goal with the Poor People's Campaign was to "focus the nation on economic inequality and poverty." Unlike the initial part of the civil rights movement, which focused on the struggles faced by African Americans, the Poor People's Campaign focused on the struggles of all minorities. King said of the campaign, "It must not be just black people, it must be all poor people. We must include American Indians, Puerto Ricans, Mexicans, and even poor whites."[2]

and his supporters wanted to make certain that the issues they represented were included in the platforms of the country's two major political parties. This meant a lot of long meetings. Those who wanted King to skip the Memphis trip thought it would detract from their work on the national political scene. King did not agree. The sanitation workers were among the people he hoped to help through the Poor People's Campaign—the working poor. King's viewpoint won out. On March 28, 1968, he traveled to Memphis to participate in a march in support of the black sanitation workers.

The March in Memphis

King's trip to Memphis did not start well. His plane was late, so he arrived after the march was planned to begin. People had gathered to participate and were eager to start the march. As they waited, their eagerness turned to impatience. By the time King arrived, thousands of protestors had gathered.

The group marched down Beale Street to Main Street. During the last few blocks of the route, the march turned into a riot of looting and physical attacks. Almost 300 African Americans were arrested. Dozens of marchers were injured and one was killed. The march had turned into chaos, becoming something very different from what King had planned and hoped for.

WORKING TOGETHER

Disappointed, King left Memphis. Critics now doubted the wisdom of having the Poor People's Campaign that King was planning in Washington, D.C. The fiasco in Memphis was proof that a peaceful march was impossible to achieve. A *New York Times* article exclaimed that the Memphis march served to "solidify white sentiment against the strikers" and that "King must by now realize that his descent on Washington is likely to prove even more counterproductive."[3]

King read and listened to the arguments against the upcoming march presented by the media. He discussed the pros and cons of the march with his advisors. He prayed. Finally, he decided that the Poor People's Campaign had to go on, but first he would return to Memphis.

King's second visit to Memphis was also delayed—by weather and a bomb threat. Late in the evening of April 3, 1968, King made his way to the pulpit of the Mason Temple. There, a crowd of 2,000 to 3,000 people—mostly sanitation workers—waited for him. King was scheduled to speak the following day, but Abernathy called King at the Lorraine Motel when he saw the size of the crowd that had turned out despite the bad weather. King spoke as he often did, in a sermon-like manner. His voice and beliefs were strong and clear: there was no standing still for the injustice taking place. Instead, they were to work together for freedom of oppression and for equality,

King, second from right, stands with other civil rights leaders on the balcony of the Lorraine Motel on April 3, 1968.

We've got to stay together and maintain unity. … We've got to give ourselves to this struggle until the end. Nothing would be more tragic than to stop at this point in Memphis. We've got to see it through. … Let us rise up tonight with a greater readiness. Let us stand with a greater determination. And let us move on in these powerful days, these days of challenge, to make America what it ought to be. We have an opportunity to make America a better nation.[5]

Death of a Dream

For most of the next day, April 4, King and some of his aides waited at the Lorraine Motel while Andrew Young and James Lawson appeared in court fighting an injunction that would prevent their march for the black sanitation workers the following Monday. When Young returned to the motel, he was grabbed by the civil rights leader and dropped to the floor. Others in the room began a pillow fight, something that might not be expected of a group of adult men fighting for the rights of an entire ethnic group. Years later, Young said that King was more playful and relaxed

The Lorraine Motel

Built during the 1920s, the Windsor Hotel was renamed the Lorraine Hotel when Walter and Loree Bailey bought it in 1942. The motel, the site of King's assassination, was added during the 1960s.

During the period of U.S. history when it was legal to restrict access on the basis of race, there were a limited number of places where black visitors could stay in Memphis. One of them was the Lorraine Motel. Located near the city's black community, the Lorraine was popular with black entertainers performing in Memphis.

After King's death, the motel fell into economic hard times and eventually was sold. It has since been turned into the National Civil Rights Museum. Visitors can see the room where King stayed and motel as they were at the time of King's assassination. Celebrities and ordinary individuals have visited the museum. On the infamous balcony where King fell, hit by an assassin's bullet, a faint stain of the leader's blood can still be seen.

that afternoon than he had been for quite some time.

King looked forward to an evening spent with friends. Ralph Abernathy, Jesse Jackson, Andrew Young, and King were going to have dinner with Reverend Billy Kyles and his wife. As the others made their way down the stairs to waiting cars, King stepped onto the balcony. Suddenly, there was a popping sound. Young thought it was a firecracker. To others, the noise sounded like a car backfiring. It was neither. A gun had been fired. Abernathy ran to the balcony and found King unconscious in a puddle of blood. He had been shot. Kyles called an ambulance. It arrived within 15 minutes and rushed King to the hospital. He had been shot in the jaw. The bullet traveled through King's body and cut his spinal cord before landing in his shoulder. He was taken

Ralph Abernathy

Ralph Abernathy was born on March 11, 1926, in Linden, Alabama. His father was a deacon in the local Baptist church. Following in his father's footsteps, Abernathy became a Baptist minister in 1948. In 1950, he received a bachelor's degree in mathematics from Alabama State College. Like King, he also studied sociology, receiving a master's degree in sociology from Atlanta University.

Abernathy first met King while a graduate student. After hearing King preach, he introduced himself. The two men became friends and partners in the fight for civil rights. When King was assassinated, Abernathy became leader of the SCLC. He resigned from the post in 1977. He served as pastor of West Hunter Street Baptist Church. In 1989, his autobiography, *And the Walls Came Tumbling Down*, was published. Ralph Abernathy died on April 17, 1990.

immediately into surgery, but the doctors could not save him. Just past 7:00 p.m., Martin Luther King Jr. was pronounced dead.

The world was about to change with the events of that night. Just a few hours after an uncharacteristically relaxed moment, the peaceful man with a powerful voice that led millions to action was silenced by an assassin's bullet. King was a husband, a father, and a minister. Growing up in the segregated South, he had experienced discrimination and inequality. These same issues had brought him to Memphis. To the disenfranchised in the United States, he was their leader, their hope. As the world learned what had happened in Memphis, many wondered if their hope of a truly desegregated country had died with King.

King's casket is being placed on a plane in Memphis to be taken to his hometown of Atlanta.

King's wife and children lead his funeral procession.

A Nation Mourns

King's death was a breaking story with few details. Most initial broadcasts reported that he had been wounded. When word came that King had died, regularly scheduled programs were interrupted on CBS, and the station logo appeared on the screen. A voiceover told viewers that King had died.

Television was different that night and for the next few nights. Once the networks learned of King's death, the rest of the evening was filled with stories about him and his work, his family, and what information there was available about the assassination and the suspect. Experts gave their opinion about how King would be remembered.

President Johnson issued a statement about King's death. Though they had not agreed on everything, the two men had worked closely together to get voting rights legislation before Congress. Johnson asked Americans to "reject the blind violence that has struck Dr. King, who lived by nonviolence."[1]

KENNEDY TELLS THE CROWD

The year 1968 was an election year. New York Senator Robert Kennedy was one of the leading candidates for the Democratic presidential nomination. Not long before he was to address a crowd of supporters in Indianapolis,

Robert Kennedy's Death

On June 6, 1968, Robert Kennedy would also fall to an assassin's bullet. One of the first people to reach out to his widow, Ethel, was Coretta Scott King.

Indiana, the senator received word of King's assassination. He asked his supporters to lower the campaign signs many of them held, saying,

> *I have some very sad news for all of you ... our fellow citizens, and people who love peace all over the world ... Martin Luther King was shot and was killed tonight in Memphis, Tennessee.*

> *Martin Luther King dedicated his life to love and to justice between fellow human beings. He died in the cause of that effort. In this difficult day ... it's perhaps well to ask what kind of a nation we are and what direction we want to move in. For those of you who are black ... you can be filled with bitterness, and with hatred, and a desire for revenge.*

"And so I say to you to-day that I still stand by nonviolence. ... I'm still convinced that it is the most potent weapon available to the Negro in his struggle for justice in this country."[3]

—Martin Luther King Jr. "Where Do We Go From Here?" annual report delivered at the eleventh convention of the SCLC August 16, 1967, Atlanta, Georgia

> *We can move in that direction as a country, in greater polarization—black people amongst blacks, and white amongst whites, filled with hatred toward one another. Or we can make an effort, as ... King did, to understand ... comprehend, and replace that violence ... across our land, with an effort to understand, compassion and love.*[2]

VIOLENCE ERUPTS

Though King had always preached peace, thousands of Americans responded to his death with violence. Television networks that had spent hours reporting about the leader who had preached nonviolence now focused on riots occurring in many of the nation's largest cities. More than 150 cities across the country reported riots. Students on many college campuses also reacted with violence.

To combat the violence, many cities enacted curfews and strictly enforced them. President Johnson

Self-defense

While King and his many followers advocated and practiced peaceful protest, not all civil rights proponents believed in such peace. Some who fought for an end to racial inequality and social and economic justice believed in using force in self-defense.

The SCLC and other organizations advocating peace were increasingly met by black nationalist leaders and newly formed militant organizations to use force. The most well-known black militant organization of the 1960s was the Black Panther Party for Self-defense, or Black Panthers. Founded in October 1966, the group believed in community and self-defense. The group received much support from young urban blacks, as well as white celebrities such as Marlon Brando and Jane Fonda. Youth supporters were easily identified by their black leather jackets and black berets. They observed police to make sure blacks were not brutalized.

The Black Panthers were watched by local police and the FBI. There was a great deal of struggle within the Black Panthers and between the organization and other groups. In addition, the Black Panther Party suffered from legal problems. These factors contributed to the group's decline in the early 1970s.

Destruction occurred as a result of riots in Washington, D.C., in response to King's death.

sent army troops and National Guardsmen to the most violent areas to curb the rioting. By April 23, 1968, 46 people had been killed and 2,600 injured in the rioting. Businesses were ransacked. Some were completely destroyed. Looting was rampant in many areas. As many as 22,000 people had been arrested, most of them for looting.

Black militant groups pushed for violence. They encouraged African Americans to retaliate against the white race for King's death. President Johnson echoed Robert Kennedy, telling Americans that fighting each other would achieve nothing. NAACP

Executive Director Roy Wilkins reminded people
that King would have hated the violence that was
being committed in his name.

THE FUNERAL

President Johnson declared April 9, the day of
King's funeral, a national day of mourning. Many
public offices, libraries, schools, and businesses
closed for the day. Rioting was replaced with
memorial parades and ceremonies—at least for
the day.

The funeral service was held in Atlanta at
Ebenezer Baptist Church, where King served as co-
pastor. His father was the pastor. Ralph Abernathy
led the service, which was attended by high-level
political and civil rights leaders. More than 60,000
people stood outside the packed church. The
service was broadcast on national
television.

King's dissertation advisor
from Boston University, L. Harold
DeWolf, described King's legacy
of love. DeWolf challenged those
assembled to carry on King's
dream:

Lester Maddox

Georgia Governor Lester
Maddox did not attend
King's funeral. He also
refused to close state government offices on that
day because he consid-
ered King an enemy of the
United States.

It is now for us ... to take up his torch of love. It is for us to finish his work ... to root out every trace of race prejudice from our lives, to bring the massive powers of this nation to aid the oppressed and to heal the hate-scarred world.[4]

King eulogized himself via a tape-recorded sermon he had given about his funeral. Coretta said it was what he wanted. He asked that the legendary singer Mahalia Jackson perform "Precious Lord, Take My Hand." She did.

Following the service, King's body was placed on a wagon drawn by two mules, a symbol of the Poor People's Campaign. Thousands of people walked behind the coffin for more than three miles (5 km) through the streets of Atlanta. After a memorial service at Morehouse College, King was laid to rest at Southview Cemetery.

King was buried and the world mourned his loss. People were eager to learn who had killed the beloved husband, father, friend, and leader. ⌐

Marchers in Memphis on April 8, 1968, in honor of King

WANTED BY THE FBI

CONSPIRACY; INTERSTATE FLIGHT - ESCAPE
JAMES EARL RAY
Photographs taken 1975

FBI No. 405,942 G

Aliases: Paul Bridgeman, Eric Starvo Galt, W. C. Herron, Harvey Lowmyer, James McBride, James O'Conner, Raymond George Sneyd, James Walton, James Walyon, John Willard, "Jim," and others.

DESCRIPTION

Age: 49, born March 10, 1928, Quincy or Alton, Illinois (not supported by birth records)
Height: 5'10"
Weight: 170 pounds
Build: Medium
Hair: Black, graying
Occupations: Baker, color matcher, laborer
Scars and Marks: Small scar on center of forehead and small scar on palm of right hand.
Remarks: Noticeably protruding left ear; reportedly a lone wolf; allegedly attended dance instruction school; reportedly completed course in bartending.
Social Security Number Used: 331-22-6876

Eyes: Blue
Complexion: Medium
Race: White
Nationality: American

An FBI wanted poster for James Earl Ray

SEARCH FOR A KILLER

*A*fter the shooting, police sectioned off a five-block area around the Lorraine Motel. Witnesses at the nearby Canipe Amusement Company reported seeing a white man run past the store. As he ran by, he dropped a package in the doorway. Shortly afterward, the witnesses saw a Mustang race by driven by the same man. The witnesses described the man as bareheaded, in his thirties, and wearing a black suit and black tie. Inside the package were a rifle with a scope and a bag containing some clothes, binoculars, beer cans, and a receipt from the York Arms Company.

IDENTIFYING A PERPETRATOR

The FBI and Memphis police investigated the murder. The shots appeared to have come from Bessie Brewer's Rooming House. John Willard, a possible match to the man witnesses had seen drop the package, had registered the afternoon of the shooting. He had been assigned to one room but asked for another. The second room had a view of the Lorraine Motel. The first room did not.

Two rooming house residents reported hearing shots coming from the vicinity of Willard's room. Both residents saw someone matching Willard's description running down the stairs and out of the building immediately following the sound of shots.

The gun and scope were traced to a store just outside of Birmingham. The gun was reportedly sold to a Harvey Lowmeyer a few days before the shooting.

A view from the window from which police believe an assassin shot King

The clerk's description of Lowmeyer was similar to the man who had registered at the rooming house.

More investigations turned up a Memphis hotel reservation the night before the shooting for Eric Starvo Galt. Galt's reservation card showed that he lived in Birmingham and drove a white Mustang. The description of Galt through his driver's license records could have described Lowmeyer, Willard, and the man who had dropped the package.

The Mustang was found in Atlanta a week after the shooting. Investigators learned the car had been serviced in Los Angeles, California. Investigators traced Galt to a school in Los Angeles. It even had a photograph of the man who called himself Eric Starvo Galt.

The FBI focused on fingerprints found in the package. This was not the suspect's first crime, and his name was not Galt, Lowmeyer, or Willard. The suspected assassin was a fugitive from the Missouri State Penitentiary named James Earl Ray.

JAMES EARL RAY

James Earl Ray was born in Alton, Illinois, on March 10, 1928. His family was poor and moved often. Ray joined the army at 17 and was sent to Germany. He started his criminal life there, though it was generally limited to drunk-and-disorderly charges. Ray spent time in the stockade, or military jail, sentenced to hard labor. When he left the army, Ray moved around. He spent a couple of nights in jail for vagrancy.

In 1949, Ray was convicted for burglary. Three years later, he received a two-year sentence for armed robbery. He was later sentenced to the federal penitentiary in Leavenworth, Kansas, for forging postal money orders.

Not long after his release from Leavenworth, Ray was sentenced to 20 years in prison for robbing a grocery store. He tried to escape in 1961 but failed. He tried again on April 23, 1967, and succeeded.

FINDING RAY

Authorities searched nationwide for Ray. They spoke to people who served time with him. A former cell mate explained that Ray had bragged about how easy it was to get a Canadian passport; that was what he was going to do when he escaped.

The FBI asked the Royal Canadian Mounted Police (RCMP) for their help in checking passport applications. The RCMP looked through 264,000 applications and found one with Ray's photo. On June 1, 1968, the FBI now had another name and more information about Ray: Ramon George Sneyd had left Toronto in

Wanted!

James Earl Ray has a distinction not shared by many criminals. He has appeared twice on the FBI's Most Wanted list. The first time was when he was identified as the primary suspect in King's murder. The FBI put Ray back on its famous list when he escaped prison in 1977.

May for the United Kingdom. Ray's life on the run ended June 8, when British authorities stopped him while trying to board a plane for Belgium.

Extradition

When a suspect is captured outside the jurisdiction in which the alleged crime occurred, an extradition procedure must take place. In the extradition process, the suspect is transferred to the jurisdiction in which the crime occurred. The person being charged with the crime can fight the extradition.

Ray was not going to return willingly to the United States to face trial for King's assassination. U.S. representatives appeared in British courts to prove that they were sure Ray had committed the crime for which he was being charged. The British courts ruled that there was

Ray's Return to the United States

Ray returned to the United States from England on an Air Force jet. Authorities did not want a repeat of the transfer of Lee Harvey Oswald, when the alleged assassin became the assassinated. Authorities in Memphis were not about to let that happen in their city.

In 1963, two days after the assassination of President John F. Kennedy, Oswald was killed as he was being transferred from Dallas Police Headquarters to the county jail. The transfer was televised, so people throughout the country witnessed Jack Ruby shoot Oswald. The shooting prevented a trial and finding Oswald guilty or innocent.

sufficient evidence to suggest that Ray had murdered King.

FINDING A LAWYER

The U.S. Constitution guarantees its citizens the right to have an attorney. Ray asked Arthur J. Hanes Sr. to represent him. Journalist William Bradford Huie offered to pay Ray $40,000 for the truth about the assassination. A portion of the money would go to Ray's attorney. Ray agreed.

RAOUL

Shortly after Ray's return to Memphis, Hanes released a statement indicating that someone other than Ray was involved in the assassination:

> *From August 1967 when he met Raoul in Montreal, down to King's death, he moved at Raoul's direction. … He delivered the rifle to Raoul … sat downstairs … waiting for Raoul. … Raoul … fired the shot … down the stairs, and threw down the rifle, zipper bag, and jumped in the Mustang where Ray was waiting, and the two drove off together.*[1]

This was the first indication that someone other than Ray was involved in the assassination. The statement explained Ray's fingerprints on the rifle and in the Mustang. Some early witnesses reported that two men had been in the car suspected of fleeing the scene. Still, authorities did not believe Ray's version of the events.

A New Lawyer

Hanes found no one to support Ray's statement about Raoul and concluded that there was no way to win the case. Hanes encouraged Ray to plead guilty in return for removing the death penalty as a possible sentence. Ray refused.

The men could not agree

Conspiracy Theories

Many people believe there was a conspiracy behind King's assassination. Some point to Ray's consistency in telling of Raoul. Others point to a lack of motive.

Journalist William Bradford Huie looks to Ray's ego as the reason. When neither his prison escape nor smuggling efforts made him famous, Huie contends that Ray had to look for bigger ways to get on the news and in the print media.

Others find it impossible to believe that Ray could have been responsible for King's death. He was simply not smart enough to carry out the assassination on his own.

One obvious consideration is radical racist groups. Conspiracy theorists also wonder about the FBI and the Central Intelligence Agency (CIA). Some suggest that the FBI or the CIA might have hired Ray to kill King.

In 1993, Lloyd Jowers claimed that mobsters paid him $100,000 to kill or arrange for the murder of King. Jowers said he worked with community members as part of the conspiracy but refused to talk about his involvement. Authorities found him not credible.

In 2002, Ronald Denton Wilson told authorities his father, Henry Clay Wilson, was behind the assassination conspiracy. His father believed King was connected with communism and wanted him dead for that reason; race was not a factor.

Percy Foreman

Percy Foreman had an impressive record as a defender of alleged murderers. By 1968, he had defended 978 individuals accused of murder. One was found guilty and executed, 53 were sent to prison, and the remainder were found not guilty.

and parted ways. In November 1968, Hanes was replaced by Percy Foreman. Foreman came to the same conclusion Hanes had. There was no way Ray was going to walk out of jail a free man. A plea bargain was reached between Ray and the prosecutors. He would plead guilty and be sentenced to 99 years in prison. There would be no trial. Ray gave a statement on March 10, 1969, in which he admitted to shooting King. He also indicated the assassination had been part of a conspiracy.

Three days later, Ray notified the case judge that he had fired his attorney and was going to recant, or take back, his confession. Ray's case went to the U.S. Supreme Court. He was refused at each step and never stood trial for King's assassination.

Ray continued to claim his innocence or at least the involvement of Raoul. He escaped from prison in 1977 and was caught three days later. Ray spent the rest of his life in prison and died in April 1998.

*A court property clerk holds the rifle thought to have been used
to kill King.*

Left to right: *Martin Luther King III, Yolanda King, Dexter King, and Coretta Scott King in 1997*

THE DREAM TODAY

The fight for civil rights in the United States did not end with the death of Dr. Martin Luther King Jr. In the years since King's assassination, legislation has been passed to strengthen and expand rights granted by the Civil Rights Act of 1964 and the 1965 Voting Rights

Act. These include laws regarding employment, education, credit, and housing.

THE CIVIL RIGHTS MOVEMENT TODAY

Today, the civil rights movement has gone beyond African Americans and whites—even race. Today's civil rights movement extends to Hispanics, Asians, homosexuals, and other minorities whose civil rights are denied. For example, the Americans with Disabilities Act, passed in 1990, guarantees that individuals with specified disabilities have access to transportation, education, employment, and health care, among other rights.

Despite these advances, much work remains to be done. At the time of his death, King was changing the direction of the civil rights movement. He knew economic equality was needed in order to have equal rights. Poverty was one of the biggest problems of King's day. It continues to be a problem and not only for African

The Martin Luther King Holiday

Not long after King's death, calls came for a national holiday in his honor. It took almost 20 years, but on November 2, 1983, President Ronald Reagan signed into federal law Martin Luther King Day. It would be observed on the third Monday of January, falling near King's birthday of January 15. The holiday was first held January 20, 1986.

Not all states were quick to add the holiday to their official calendars. It was not until January 17, 2000, that the holiday was observed in all 50 states.

Americans. With inspiration drawn from King and others who fought for civil rights during the 1950s and 1960s, many people and organizations continue to work toward eliminating this form of inequality, including King's widow and children.

KING'S FAMILY

King's wife and children followed in his footsteps in various ways. Coretta Scott King had always supported her husband and his cause. She continued to do so after his death. In 1968, she established the King Center in

---

A Life Not Lived in Vain

Every now and then I think about my own death ... I'd like somebody to mention that day, that Martin Luther King, Jr., tried to give his life serving others ... to love somebody ... to be right on the war question ... to feed the hungry ... to clothe those who were naked ... to visit those who were in prison.

I want you to say that I tried to love and serve humanity.

Yes, if you want to say that I was a drum major, say that I was a drum major for justice. ... for peace. ... for righteousness. And all of the other shallow things will not matter. I won't have any money to leave behind. ... But I just want to leave a committed life behind. And that's all I want to say.

If I can help somebody as I pass along, if I can cheer somebody with a word or song, if I can show somebody he's traveling wrong, then my living will not be in vain. ...[1]

—Martin Luther King Jr.
"Drum major instinct"
February 4, 1968

Atlanta. The center is in the Martin Luther King Jr. National Historic Site.

Until a stroke limited her ability to speak and her subsequent death in 2006, Coretta Scott King was a tireless fighter on behalf of civil rights. She fought against South Africa's policy of apartheid and against capital punishment. She stood in support of world peace, gay rights, feminism, and HIV/AIDS prevention. She wrote three books and received more than 60 honorary degrees. She also served as an example to her four children.

Yolanda King, the oldest of the King children, graduated from Smith College and earned a master's degree from New York University. She was a human rights activist and actress, starring as Rosa Parks in the television miniseries *King*. Yolanda was a vocal activist for gay rights. She actively supported Habitat for Humanity and was the spokesperson for the National Stroke Awareness Association. Yolanda died unexpectedly in 2007.

Martin Luther King III served as an elected official in Georgia and as head of the SCLC and the King Center. Today, he heads Realizing the Dream, Inc., which he founded in 2006. The organization promotes justice, equality, and community

King in London

King's importance in history is recognized beyond the United States. Above the Great West Door of London's famous Westminster Abbey is a statue of King. He is included among the ten twentieth-century martyrs from across the world.

through economic development, nonviolence and conflict resolution training, and targeted leadership development programs for youth.

Just as his father had done, Dexter King attended Morehouse College, though he did not graduate. He has worked as an actor and documentary filmmaker. Named after the Dexter Avenue Baptist Church, Dexter has been quite vocal in his belief that James Earl Ray did not kill his father, even meeting with the convicted murderer.

Bernice King followed in her father's footsteps by becoming a minister. She graduated from Spelman College and has a master's degree in divinity and a doctorate in law from Emory University. Bernice has not always agreed with the views of her family, becoming an outspoken opponent of gay rights. She established a scholarship in her mother's honor at Spelman College.

HE BELONGS TO THE AGES

While questions and debate about King's death remain, his life shows certainty. On March 22, 1959,

King gave a sermon on Gandhi:

The world doesn't like people like Gandhi. That's strange, isn't it? They don't like people like Christ; they don't like people like Lincoln. They killed him—this man who had done all of that for India, who gave his life and who mobilized and galvanized 400 million people for independence. … One of his own fellow Hindus felt that he was a little too favorable toward the Moslems, felt that he was giving in too much for the Moslems. … here was the man of nonviolence, falling at the hands of a man of violence. Here was a man of love falling at the hands of a man with hate. This seems the way of history. And isn't it significant that he died on the same day that Christ died? It was on Friday. And this is the story of history, but thank God it never stopped here. Thank God Good Friday is never the end. The man who shot Gandhi only shot him into the hearts of humanity. Just as when Abraham Lincoln was shot, mark you, for the same reason that Mahatma Gandhi was shot—that is, the attempt to heal the wounds of the divided nation—when Abraham Lincoln was shot, Secretary Stanton stood by and said, "Now he belongs to the ages." The same thing could be said about Mahatma Gandhi now: He belongs to the ages.[2]

King's words about Gandhi apply to himself. A man of love, King fell at the hands of a man of hate.

MLK Papers Project

In 1985, Coretta Scott King contacted Clayborne Carson, a historian at Stanford University. She was looking for someone to edit and publish a collection of her late husband's papers. With that, the Martin Luther King Jr. Papers Project of the Martin Luther King Jr. Research and Education Institute was established. The goal of the project is to publish a 14-volume collection of the civil rights leader's speeches, sermons, and other writings.

His shooting shot him into the hearts of humanity. King's life is an example of what one person can do with faith, hope, determination, and devotion. And while we will never know what else King would have done in his life, the successes of his life are clear. He inspired individuals, groups, an entire race, and a country. His words and work have affected countless lives—and continue to do so today, almost four decades since his assassination. King belongs to the ages.

King's crypt

TIMELINE

1929	1953	1954
Martin Luther King Jr. is born in Atlanta, Georgia, on January 15.	King and Coretta Scott marry on June 18.	On May 17, the U.S. Supreme Court rules in *Brown v. Board of Education* that segregation in public schools is illegal and must end.

1957	1957	1958
On January 10, the SCLC forms to coordinate civil rights protest efforts in the South.	King leads a prayer pilgrimage to Washington, D.C., on May 17.	On September 20, King is stabbed at a book signing.

1955

On December 1, Rosa Parks refuses to give up her bus seat, setting the stage for the Montgomery bus boycott.

1956

On November 13, the U.S. Supreme Court affirms the lower court ruling that segregation on public transportation is unconstitutional.

1956

After 381 days, the Montgomery bus boycott ends on December 21.

1961

Freedom Riders are attacked in Alabama on May 14.

1963

King writes his "Letter from Birmingham Jail" on April 16.

1963

More than 200,000 people attend the March on Washington on August 28. King concludes with his "I have a dream" speech.

TIMELINE

1963	1964	1964
Four African-American girls are killed on September 15 in a church bombing in Birmingham.	On July 2, President Johnson signs the Civil Rights Act of 1964 into law.	King accepts his Nobel Peace Prize on December 10.

1968	1968	1969
King is buried on April 9, a national day of mourning.	James Earl Ray is arrested on June 8 for King's murder.	On March 10, Ray pleads guilty to killing King.

1965	1968	1968
Troopers and local officers attack participants on March 7 in the Selma march, now known as "Bloody Sunday."	King gives his "I've been to the mountaintop" speech on April 3 in support of striking sanitation workers.	King is assassinated in Memphis, Tennessee, on April 4.

1998	2006	2007
Ray dies of liver disease in prison on April 23.	Coretta Scott King dies on January 30.	Yolanda King dies on May 15.

Essential Facts

Date of Event

April 4, 1968

Place of Event

Memphis, Tennessee

Key Players

❖ Martin Luther King Jr.

❖ James Earl Ray

Highlights of Event

❖ Martin Luther King Jr. led the civil rights movement in the 1950s and 1960s.

❖ Black sanitation workers in Memphis, Tennessee, went on strike in 1968.

❖ Martin Luther King Jr. was assassinated on April 4, 1968, while in Memphis supporting the sanitation workers.

❖ King was buried on April 9, 1968. President Johnson declared a national day of mourning.

❖ James Earl Ray was arrested in Great Britain on June 8, 1968, for King's assassination.

❖ On March 10, 1969, Ray pleaded guilty to the assassination but claimed it was part of a conspiracy.

Quote

"Martin Luther King dedicated his life to love and to justice between fellow human beings. He died in the cause of that effort. In this difficult day ... it's perhaps well to ask what kind of a nation we are and what direction we want to move in. For those of you who are black ... you can be filled with bitterness, and with hatred, and a desire for revenge.

We can move in that direction as a country, in greater polarization—black people amongst blacks, and white amongst whites, filled with hatred toward one another. Or we can make an effort, as ... King did, to understand ... comprehend, and replace that violence ... across our land, with an effort to understand, compassion and love." —*Robert F. Kennedy, on announcing the death of King*

ADDITIONAL RESOURCES

SELECT BIBLIOGRAPHY

Branch, Taylor. *Parting the Waters: America in the King Years 1954–63*. New York: Simon and Schuster, 1988.

Branch, Taylor. *Pillar of Fire: America in the King Years 1963–65*. New York: Simon and Schuster, 1998.

Bullard, Sara, ed. *Free at Last: A History of the Civil Rights Movement & Those Who Died in the Struggle*. Montgomery, AL: Teaching Tolerance, Southern Poverty Law Center, 2004.

Fitzgerald, Stephanie. *Struggling for Civil Rights*. Chicago: Raintree, 2006.

Ritchie, Nigel. *The Civil Rights Movement*. Hauppauge, NY: Barron's Educational Series, Inc., 2002.

FURTHER READING

Ching, Jacqueline. *The Assassination of Martin Luther King, Jr.* New York: Rosen, 2002.

Posner, Gerald. *Killing the Dream: James Earl Ray and the Assassination of Martin Luther King Jr.* New York: Harvest Books, 1999.

Supples, Kevin. *Speaking Out: The Civil Rights Movement 1950–1964*. Washington, DC: National Geographic Society, 2002.

WEB LINKS

To learn more about the assassination of Martin Luther King Jr., visit ABDO Publishing Company on the World Wide Web at **www.abdopublishing.com**. Web sites about the assassination of Martin Luther King Jr. are featured on our Book Links page. These links are routinely monitored and updated to provide the most current information available.

Places To Visit

The Civil Rights Memorial

402 Washington Avenue, Montgomery, AL 36104

334-956-8200

www.spelcenter.org

The memorial honors those who have lost their lives in the pursuit of civil rights. The marble disk bears the names and dates of important events in the struggle, and one of King's most memorable quotes is engraved on the wall behind it. The visitor center provides a more in-depth examination of the civil rights movement, past and present.

The King Center

449 Auburn Avenue Northeast, Atlanta, GA 30312

404-526-8900

www.thekingcenter.org

The center, which resides in the Martin Luther King Jr. National Historic Site along with King's childhood home, is responsible for administering many programs and serving as a research center.

National Civil Rights Museum

450 Mulberry Street, Memphis, TN 38103

901-521-9699

www.civilrightsmuseum.org

Housed in the former Lorraine Motel, the site of King's assassination, the museum commemorates the event and other lives and events that define the civil rights movement.

GLOSSARY

advocate
Someone who supports a belief, cause, or person.

alleged
Claimed but not yet proven.

boycott
A form of protest in which a decision is made not to deal with a company or an organization.

civil disobedience
The nonviolent, purposeful violation of certain laws that a person believes are wrong.

conspiracy
A secret plan by two or more people, often to do something illegal or harmful.

disenfranchised
Those denied a privilege or a legal right, particularly the right to vote.

divinity
A study of religion.

extradition
The taking of an alleged criminal from one jurisdiction to another—most likely the one in which the alleged crime occurred—so that the person can be tried for the crime he or she is accused of committing.

HIV/AIDS
HIV stands for human immunodeficiency virus and is the retrovirus that causes AIDS, which is acquired immune deficiency syndrome. HIV/AIDS severely affects the body's immune system.

indictment
Formal accusation of a serious crime.

injunction
A court order that requires someone to do or not to do something.

Jim Crow
A term applied to practices that discriminate against African Americans.

jurisdiction
The territory in which a law applies.

legacy
Something that passes from one generation to the next.

mesmerize
To fascinate; to get someone's complete attention.

oppression
The act of subjecting someone to harsh or cruel domination.

pastorate
The area over which a pastor is responsible.

prejudice
Unfounded negative feelings or beliefs about a group of people based on race, religion, or nationality.

retaliate
To deliberately harm someone in response to something he or she has done.

segregate
To separate one group from another one, often on the basis of race.

sit-in
A form of protest in which people occupy a public place and refuse to leave until their demands are met.

strike
To not work in order to make an employer behave in a particular way, meet a demand.

theology
The study of religion.

Source Notes

Chapter 1. I See the Promised Land

1.Martin Luther King, Jr. "I've Been to the Mountaintop." Bishop
Charles J. Mason Temple, Memphis, Tennessee. 3 April, 1968. *Martin
Luther King Papers Project*. Stanford University. 16 Nov. 2007
<http://www.stanford.edu/group/King/publications/speeches/
I've_been_to_the_mountaintop.pdf>.

2. Ibid.

3. "Quick Guide & Transcript: Review the week's headlines, Reflect on
the last days of MLK." *CNN.com*. Cable Network News. 2007. 16 Nov.
2007 <http://www.cnn.com/2007/EDUCATION/01/18/transcript.fri/
index.html>.

4. Martin Luther King, Jr. "I've Been to the Mountaintop." Bishop
Charles J. Mason Temple, Memphis, Tennessee. 3 April, 1968. *Martin
Luther King Papers Project*. Stanford University. 16 Nov. 2007
<http://www.stanford.edu/group/King/publications/speeches/I've_been_
to_the_mountaintop.pdf>.

Chapter 2. Young Martin

1. Martin Luther King, Jr. *The Autobiography of Martin Luther King, Jr*. Ed.
Clayborne Carson. New York: Warner Books, 1998. 4.

2. Ibid. 9–10.

3. Ibid. 10.

Chapter 3. Becoming a Leader

1. Martin Luther King, Jr. "Address to First Montgomery Improvement
Association (MIA) Mass Meeting." Holt Street Baptist Church,
Montgomery, Alabama. 5. Dec. 1955. *Martin Luther King Papers Project*.
Stanford University. 16 Nov. 2007 <http://www.stanford.edu/group/
King/publications/speeches/MIA_mass_meeting_at_holt_street.html>.

2. Ibid.

3. Clayborne Carson, Stewart Burns, Susan Carson, Pete Holloran, and
Dana Powell, eds. *The Papers of Martin Luther King, Volume III: Birth of a New Age,
December 1955–December 1956*. Berkeley, CA: University of California Press,
1997. 114–115.

4. Martin Luther King, Jr. *The Autobiography of Martin Luther King, Jr*. Ed.
Clayborne Carson. New York: Warner Books, 1998. 78.

Chapter 4. I Have a Dream

1. Martin Luther King, Jr. *The Autobiography of Martin Luther King, Jr*.
Ed. Clayborne Carson. New York: Warner Books, 1998. 140.

2. Ibid. 188–189.

3. Nigel Ritchie. *The Civil Rights Movement*. Hauppauge, NY: Barron's

Educational Series, Inc., 2002. 28.
4. Martin Luther King, Jr. "I Have a Dream" Address delivered at
the March on Washington for Jobs and Freedom. Washington, DC.
28 Aug. 1963. *Martin Luther King Papers Project*. Stanford University.
25 Nov. 2007 <http://www.stanford.edu/group/King/publications/
speeches/address_at_march_on_washington.pdf>.
5. Ibid.
6. "Selma to Montgomery March." *King Encyclopedia*, Stanford University.
16 Nov. 2007 <http://www.stanford.edu/group/King/about_king/
encyclopedia/selma_montgomery.htm>.

Chapter 5. We Shall Overcome
1. Martin Luther King, Jr. *The Autobiography of Martin Luther King, Jr.* Ed.
Clayborne Carson. New York: Warner Books, 1998. 77.
2. Ibid. 229.
3. Philip Nel. "We Shall Overcome." *A Brief History of Music and Race in Twentieth
Century America*, Kansas State University. 18 Nov. 2007
<http://www.k-state.edu/english/nelp/american.studies.s98/we.shall.
overcome.html>.
4. Jules Archer. *They Had a Dream: The Civil Rights Struggle from Frederick Douglass to
Marcus Garvey to Martin Luther King and Malcolm X.* New York: Penguin Books,
1993. 139.
5. Martin Luther King, Jr. *The Autobiography of Martin Luther King, Jr.* Ed.
Clayborne Carson. New York: Warner Books, 1998. 141.
6. Ibid.
7. "Selma to Montgomery March." *King Encyclopedia*, Stanford University.
20 Nov. 2007 <http://www.stanford.edu/group/King/about_king/
encyclopedia/selma_montgomery.htm>.
8. Martin Luther King, Jr. *The Autobiography of Martin Luther King, Jr.* Ed.
Clayborne Carson. New York: Warner Books, 1998. 63.

Chapter 6. Shots Fired
1. Martin Luther King, Jr. *The Autobiography of Martin Luther King, Jr.* Ed.
Clayborne Carson. New York: Warner Books, 1998. 346.
2. "Poor People's Campaign." *King Encyclopedia*, Stanford University.
16 Nov. 2007 <http://www.stanford.edu/group/King/about_king/
encyclopedia/poorpeoples.html>.
3. Taylor Branch. *At Canaan's Edge: America in the King Years 1965–68.* New York:
Simon and Schuster, 2006. 744.
4. Martin Luther King, Jr. *The Autobiography of Martin Luther King, Jr.* Ed.
Clayborne Carson. New York: Warner Books, 1998. 349.
5. Ibid. 360–361.

Source Notes Continued

Chapter 7. A Nation Mourns
1. Lyndon B. Johnson. Statement by the President on the Assassination of Dr. Martin Luther King, Jr. White House, Washington, DC. 4 April 1968. *The American Presidency Project*. Ed. Gerhard Peters and John T. Woolley. 2007. 25 Nov. 2007 <http://www.presidency.ucsb.edu/ws/index. php?pid=28781>.
2. Robert F. Kennedy. Remarks on the Assassination of Martin Luther King, Jr. Indianapolis, Indiana, April 4, 1968. *AmericanRhetoric.com*. 2007. American Rhetoric. 18 Nov. 2007 <http://www.americanrhetoric.com/ speeches/rfkonmlkdeath.html>.
3. Martin Luther King, Jr. "Where Do We Go from Here." Atlanta, Georgia. 16 Aug. 1967. *Martin Luther King Papers Project*. Stanford University. 18 Nov. 2007 <http://www.stanford.edu/group/King/publications/ speeches/Where_do_we_go_from_here.html>.
4. L. Howard DeWolf. "Funeral Tribute to Martin Luther King, Jr., *Religion & Ethics Newsweekly*. 13 Jan. 2006. <http://www.pbs.org/wnet/ religionandethics/week920/tribute.html>.
5. Martin Luther King, Jr. Epitaph, South View Cemetery, Atlanta, Georgia.

Chapter 8. Search for a Killer
1. "James Earl Ray: The Man Who Killed Dr. Martin Luther King Jr.: The Plea." *CrimeLibrary.com*. 2007 Turner Entertainment Digital Network, Inc. 18 Nov. 2007 <http://www.crimelibrary.com/terrorists_spies/ assassins/ray/11.html>.

Chapter 9. The Dream Today
1. Martin Luther King, Jr. "The Drum Major Instinct." Ebenezer Baptist Church, Atlanta, Georgia. 4 Feb. 1968. *Martin Luther King Papers Project*, Stanford University. 18 Nov. 2007 <http://www.stanford.edu/group/ King/publications/sermons/680204.000_Drum_Major_Instinct.html>.
2. Clayborne Carson, Tenisha Armstrong, Susan Carson, Adrienne Clay, and Kieran Taylor, eds. *The Papers of Martin Luther King, Volume 5: Threshold of a New Decade, January 1959–December 1960*. Berkeley, CA: University of California Press, 2005. 145–157.

INDEX

About the Author

Ida Walker is the author of several nonfiction books for middle-grade and young-adult readers. Her special interest is the civil rights movement of the 1960s, and she has visited many of the locations of the memorable events of the movement. She lives in upstate New York.

Photo Credits

AP Images, cover, 3, 16, 27, 37, 38, 49, 59, 60, 65, 69, 70, 74, 77, 78, 80, 96 (top), 98 (top), 99; Bettmann/Corbis, 9, 55, 56; Charles Kelly/AP Images, 15, 96 (bottom) ; Corbis, 21; Horace Cort/AP Images, 28, 44, 97; Gene Herrick/AP Images, 50; John L. Focht/AP Images, 87; Alan Mothner/AP Images, 88; John Bazemore/AP Images, 95, 98 (bottom)